COOL PETS
for Kids

Fish

DAWN TITMUS

PowerKiDS
press™

Published in 2019 by The Rosen
Publishing Group, Inc.
29 East 21st Street, New York, NY 10010

Cataloging-in-Publication Data

Names: Titmus, Dawn.
Title: Fish / Dawn Titmus.
Description: New York : PowerKids Press, 2019. | Series: Cool pets for kids | Includes glossary and index.
Identifiers: LCCN ISBN 9781538338759 (pbk.) | ISBN 9781538338742 (library bound) |
ISBN 9781538338766 (6 pack)
Subjects: LCSH: Aquarium fishes--Juvenile literature. | Pets--Juvenile literature.
Classification: LCC SF457.25 T58 2019 | DDC 639.8--dc23

Copyright © 2019 BROWN BEAR BOOKS LTD

Text and editor: Dawn Titmus
Editorial Director: Lindsey Lowe
Children's Publisher: Anne O'Daly
Design Manager: Keith Davis
Picture Manager: Sophie Mortimer

Photo acknowledgements:
t=top, c=center, b=bottom, l=left, r=right
Interior: Alamy: blickwinkel/Schmidbauer 25b, Photononstop 17; Dreamstime: Mikhailg 21t, 26–27; iStock: b_ial_y 20, EuToch 19b, FamVeld 11t, isoft 24, mtreasure 5, 21b, rclassenlayouts 18, vlado1 14–15, 15; Shutterstock: 12photography 10t, anmbph 9t, Jovan Barajevac 12, bluehand 23t, Chaikom 4, cynoclub 3, 4–5, 6, ET19727t, FamVeld 12–13, Elena Frolova 29b, Alexander Geiger 9b, Iliuta Goean 22, Andrea Izzotti 29t, CO Leong 14, Kazakov Maksim 27b, Grigorev Mikhail 16–17t, MyStocks 1, Oleg_P 19t, Peyker 7b, Mirko Rosenau 10bl, 10br, 11b, 13, 27t, Kocsis Sandor 23b, 25t, set 16–17b, showcake 8–9b, Vlad61 29c, Suttipon Yakham 10c; Thinkstock: mauriziobiso 8-9t.

Manufactured in the United States of America

CPSIA Compliance Information: Batch #CS18PK: For Further Information contact Rosen Publishing, New York, New York at 1-800-237-9932.

Contents

Which Fish?

Looking after fish can be an exciting hobby. Fish come in all shapes and sizes and in an impressive range of colors. Keeping fish in a tank gives a fascinating glimpse into their underwater world.

Coldwater or Tropical?

Coldwater fish and tropical fish have different care needs. Goldfish are coldwater fish. They can live in water that is the same temperature as the rooms in most homes. Tropical fish, such as tetras, come from hot regions of the world. The water in their tank needs to be warm for the fish to survive.

Space and Time

Do you have space and time to keep and look after fish? The tank needs to be in the right position. Place it away from direct heat sources, such as a sunny window or radiator, and drafty areas. Put the tank on a firm, flat surface raised off the floor. You'll need to spend time cleaning the tank. The water will need to be changed regularly, too.

A Community Aquarium

Some fish like to be with their own type of fish. Others can live with different species. When different fish are kept in one tank, it is called a community aquarium. Guppies, southern platies, and mollies can all live happily with other types of fish.

The Right Fish for You?

☑ Do you want to keep coldwater or tropical fish?

☑ Have you researched how to look after the fish you want to keep?

☑ Do you have the space for a fish tank?

☑ Do you have time to clean the tank and change the water regularly?

☑ Can your family afford to buy the equipment?

Read On ...

Fish are great pets and are fascinating to watch, but it is important to choose the right ones for you. This book will help you to pick and care for your pet. Learn about six fish that are among the easiest to care for. Try your hand at making a Jell-O aquarium. You will also find some fascinating facts about your new fishy friends!

What You Will Need

The tank is the most important item you will need for your fish. Keeping the water clean and at the correct temperature is important for the health of your pet.

Checklist

- ☑ A tank the right size for your fish.
- ☑ Heater and thermostat for tropical fish.
- ☑ A filter the right size for the tank.
- ☑ Tank ornaments and water plants.
- ☑ Tank gravel.
- ☑ Gravel cleaner (siphon set).
- ☑ Air pump (optional).

The Tank

Fish need room to swim. Once you have decided on the type of fish you want to keep, buy a tank big enough for that type. Don't buy fish that will outgrow the tank. Start with a 20-gallon (75 liter) tank. Line the bottom of the tank with gravel. You will need a gravel cleaner (siphon set) for cleaning the tank.

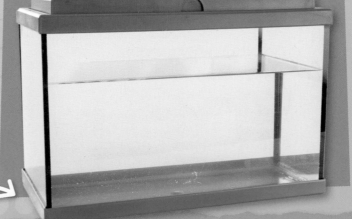

Tank

Filter and Air Pump

Fish poop ends up in the water. Fish in a tank cannot swim to a cleaner place if the water gets dirty. That is why it is important to filter the water for all types of fish. Set up a filter that is the right size for your tank. Change the filter material regularly. You can also install an air pump to get more oxygen into the water.

Heating the Water

Tropical fish need the water to be at higher temperatures than for coldwater fish. Most tropical fish are happiest in water that is between 75 and 82 °F (24 and 28 °C). Use a heater with a thermostat to keep the water at the correct temperature for your fish.

Air pump

Filter

Water heater

Gravel

Plants and Ornaments

Plants and ornaments in the tank look attractive and also provide shelter, hiding places, and shade for your fish. Some fish nibble on water plants, so you will have to replace them from time to time. Be sure to use aquatic ornaments that are safe for fish.

The Tank

Before you bring any fish home, it is important to prepare the tank properly. Clean it regularly to keep your fish happy in their new home.

Preparing the Tank

Water from the faucet contains chemicals that are harmful to fish. The tank filter also needs to grow some "good" bacteria. You can buy products at the pet store that remove chemicals from tap water and help good bacteria grow. Rinse the gravel with water and add it to the tank. Fill the tank with water and add the ornaments and plants. Turn on all the equipment. Run it for at least three days before you introduce fish to the tank. Make sure the water temperature is right for your type of fish.

Testing Kits

You can buy testing kits for the water at the pet store. Test the water for harmful chemicals before you add any fish. Some fish stores will test a sample of tank water for you. Test the water regularly when your tank contains fish. If the chemical levels are too high, you need to change the water.

Fresh Water

The tank water needs to be changed about once a week. Remove 15 to 20 percent of the water using a siphon. Top up the tank with water that has been treated to remove harmful chemicals.

Siphon

Keeping It Clean

Check all equipment every day. If there is uneaten food and waste in the tank, take it out with a net. Scrub off any algae growing on the side of the tank. Clean or change the filter regularly. Use water from the aquarium to wash the filter. Tap water contains bacteria that is harmful to fish. Never use any detergents to clean the tank as they can harm the fish.

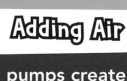

Adding Air

Air pumps create bubbles. This moves the water around and gets more oxygen into the water, which is good for your fish. It's also fun to watch your fish swim through bubbles!

Feeding Time

Different types of fish need different types of food. Ask at the pet store what the best diet is for your fish and how much to feed them. The right amount is important for your fish to thrive.

Fishy Food

Fish food includes flakes and pellets for plant and meat eaters, and freeze-dried food. Some fish such as catfish feed from the bottom of the tank. They need food that will sink. Fish that feed at the surface, such as hatchetfish, need food that will float, such as flakes or floating pellets.

Flakes

Pellets

Freeze-dried food

Extra Treats

Give your fish other types of food as well as flakes for a balanced diet. Goldfish will eat chopped-up spinach or lettuce. Some types of tropical fish like crumbled egg yolk. Meat-eating fish, such as swordtails, need small live food, such as brine shrimp. You can also buy it frozen in fish stores.

Keeping It Fresh

Check the sell-by date on fish food before you buy. Food that is out of date can lack vitamins. Keep the food in an airtight container, away from heat and light. Make sure no water gets into the food container. Even a small amount of moisture can cause harmful bacteria to grow in the food.

The Right Amount

Most fish need to be fed once or twice every day. Feed only as much as the fish eat in a few minutes. Giving your fish too much food is bad for them. Food that is uneaten will go stale, making the water unhealthy. Your filter system will have to work harder to keep the water clean. You will also have to change the water more often. It is better to feed too little to start with, rather than too much.

Staying Healthy

Providing your fish with plenty of space, a clean tank and water, and the right amount of food will help keep them healthy. Check your fish every day for signs of sickness.

Healthy Fish

Healthy fish eat their food and are active and alert. Their eyes are bright and clear. The gills open and close regularly, and their fins do not have any splits or tears. Watch for signs of sickness in your fish. Take it to the vet if you think it is sick.

A New Home

Once the tank is all set up and working properly, you can slowly introduce the fish. Leave the fish in the bag you brought it home in. Float the bag in the tank so the fish gets used to the temperature. You can put a little of the tank water in the bag after about 20 minutes. After about 30 minutes, let the fish swim into the tank. Throw away the water that was in the bag.

Plenty of Space

Be careful not to put too many fish into your tank. Overcrowding will stress the fish and can make them sick. Your filter will also have to work a lot harder to keep the water clean. A general rule is 1 inch (2.5 cm) of fish length per gallon (3.8 liters) of water. Plants and ornaments take up space, too. Put fewer fish in the tank than you think it can hold.

A Happy Home

Check that the water temperature is right for your pet. Use a test kit to check for harmful chemicals and change the water regularly. Only leave tank lights on for 8 to 10 hours a day. Fish need down time!

Carefully introduce fish to the tank.

Signs of Sickness

- ✔ Gasping at the surface.
- ✔ Swimming at an angle.
- ✔ Injuries or lumps on the scales.
- ✔ Pale patches on the scales.
- ✔ White spots.
- ✔ White tufts like cotton balls.

In the Wild

Fish live almost everywhere in the world. They live in freshwater, seawater, and brackish water, which is slightly salty. Most fish kept as pets in aquariums live in freshwater in the wild—in rivers, lakes, and streams.

South America

Many types of aquarium fish come from South America. These include the tetras and red-bellied piranhas (below). Rivers and streams in South America range from clear, uncolored waters to the black water of the Rio Negro in the Amazon basin. Around 3,000 different types of fish live in the Amazon basin.

African Rift Lakes

The African Rift Lakes are in eastern Africa. They are among the largest and deepest lakes in the world. More than 1,500 different types of fish live in the lakes. Some, such as the Malawi golden cichlid, are found nowhere else in the world.

Schooling Fish

In the wild, some fish, such as danios, swim together in groups, called schools. Individual fish in a large group have less chance of being eaten by a predator than if they are swimming alone. Schooling fish need to have tank mates of their own kind. If they are alone, they will become nervous and stressed. Schooling fish usually live happily with other types of fish in a community aquarium.

Friends and Enemies

Some fish, such as the dwarf gourami, live happily with other types of fish, as they would in the wild. Other fish are not suitable for a community aquarium. Oscars and angelfish (right) eat other smaller fish in the wild. Bettas (Siamese fighting fish) are territorial in the wild. Male bettas are very aggressive toward each other and should not be kept in the same tank. But bettas can be kept with peaceful fish, such as tetras.

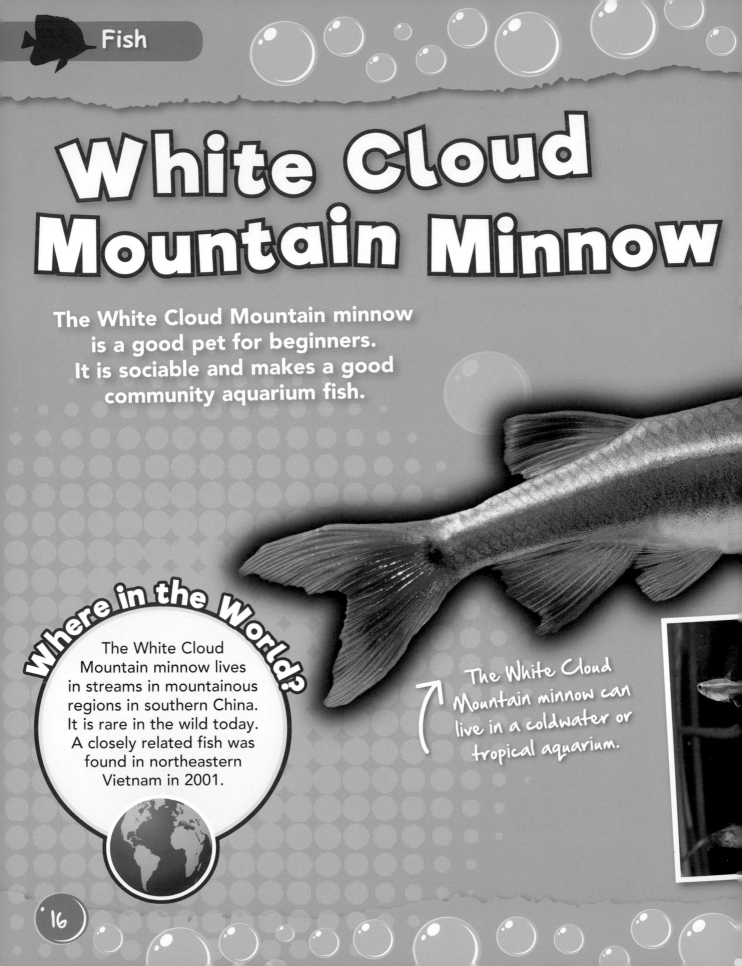

White Cloud Mountain Minnow

The White Cloud Mountain minnow is a good pet for beginners. It is sociable and makes a good community aquarium fish.

Where in the World?

The White Cloud Mountain minnow lives in streams in mountainous regions in southern China. It is rare in the wild today. A closely related fish was found in northeastern Vietnam in 2001.

The White Cloud Mountain minnow can live in a coldwater or tropical aquarium.

Breed Profile

The White Cloud Mountain minnow grows to about 1.75 inches (4.5 cm) long. An iridescent line runs along the body. Males have red-colored fins. There are gold (right) and long-finned types. All types of minnow can live for up to four or five years.

Looking After Me

White Cloud Mountain minnows are schooling fish. Keep them in groups of at least five fish.

☑ They can live in water temperatures as low as 64 °F (18 °C) and up to about 72 °F (22 °C).

☑ They feed on flakes with lots of vegetables and frozen foods such as brine shrimp and blood worms.

Goldfish

Goldfish are among the most popular aquarium fish. They come in many different sizes and colors.

Where in the World?

Goldfish come from China. They were first kept as pets about 1,000 years ago. They were taken to Japan in the 1500s and were introduced to Europe in the 1700s.

There are about 150 different types of goldfish.

Breed Profile

The goldfish is a member of the carp family. Depending on the type, goldfish grow to about 12 inches (30 cm) long, but some are smaller. Fancy goldfish need greater care than common goldfish. Goldfish live for about six to eight years, but some may live much longer.

Looking After Me

Goldfish do not need a water heater unless the room is very cold. The water temperature can be between 65 and 77 °F (18 and 25 °C).

☑ Goldfish can live in a tank by themselves or with others. Comet and fancy goldfish are not good tank mates. The comets swim faster and get to the food first.

☑ Goldfish will eat most food types. Feed them quality flakes or pellets made especially for goldfish.

Neon Tetra

The tropical neon tetra is one of the most popular pet fish. It has beautiful bright colors, is a peaceful fish, and is one of the easiest to care for.

Where in the World?

The neon tetra originally came from rivers and streams in rain forests in Colombia, Peru, and Brazil. It is often found in blackwater streams, where its bright colors make it stand out.

Neon tetras will live happily in a tank with other fish.

Breed Profile

The neon tetra has a silver-white body. It has a blue stripe that runs along its body from its nose to just past its back fin. It also has a red stripe that starts in the middle of the body and ends at the tail fin. Tetras grow to about 1.2 inches (3 cm) in length. Females are slightly larger than males. Neon tetras live for 10 or more years.

Looking After Me

Neon tetras are schooling fish, so keep them in groups of at least five fish.

☑ Keep the water temperature in the tank at about 68 to 79 °F (20 to 26 °C).

☑ Neon tetras feed on regular flake food and pellets, as well as on frozen and live food.

Molly Fish

Mollies are a great community aquarium fish. They are easy to care for and come in numerous varieties. The females give birth to live young rather than laying eggs.

Where in the World?

In the wild, mollies live in freshwater streams and in brackish and coastal waters from Texas to Mexico. Some are found in waters in Colombia and Venezuela.

The molly is a peaceful fish.

Mollies are available in many different colors, shapes, and patterns. The black molly is one of the most popular. Other types are the gold dust molly, which is yellow and orange, and the black-and-white dalmatian molly. Females grow to about 4.5 inches (12 cm), and males grow to 3 inches (8 cm). They live for three to five years.

Looking After Me

Mollies like company. Keep at least one male and two females together, or a group of females if you don't want them to breed.

☑ The water in the tank can be fresh or brackish—with a little salt added. Keep the temperature around 77 to 82 °F (25 to 28 °C).

☑ Mollies will feed on algae, flakes, and frozen and dried food.

Guppy

Guppies come in a huge range of colors, fin types, and patterns. They are active swimmers, making them fun to watch. The females give birth to live young.

Where in the World?

Guppies live in the waters of Venezuela, Brazil, and some Caribbean islands. They eat insects and have been introduced to other parts of the world to try to reduce mosquito populations.

Guppies are also known as rainbow fish and millions fish.

Breed Profile

Male guppies are more colorful than females, often with long, flowing tail fins. Guppy colors include yellow, red, blue, and purple. There are also patterned types such as snakeskin and lace guppies. Females grow to about 2 inches (5 cm) and are double the size of the males. Guppies live for three to five years.

Looking After Me

Guppies are active tropical fish and need plenty of space to swim. They also like plants to nibble on.

- ☑ The temperature of the water should be around 64 to 82 °F (18 to 28 °C).

- ☑ Feed guppies flake food. Pellets are too large for their mouths. They also feed on live or frozen food such as brine shrimp.

Zebra Danio

Zebra danios are active swimmers and are ideal for a first aquarium. Breeding pairs have a strong bond and will mate for life.

Where in the World?

In the wild, zebra danios are found in rivers and streams of the Ganges Delta region in eastern India and Bangladesh.

The zebra danio gets its name from the stripes on its body, which look like zebra stripes.

Breed Profile

Zebra danios have dark horizontal stripes running the length of the body. Females are larger than males and have silver bodies. Males have gold bodies. Other types include the leopard danio (left), which has more spotted patterning, and some types have long fins. Danios grow to about 2 inches (5 cm) in length and live for about three to five years.

Looking After Me

Zebra danios like to live in a school of at least five fish. Good tank mates include rainbowfish, platies, mollies, and swordtails.

☑ The temperature of the water should be around 64 to 75 °F (18 to 24 °C).

☑ Feed zebra danios flake food and freeze-dried food such as blood worms and brine shrimp.

Make It!
Jell-O Aquarium

Use some Jell-O and candy to make this fishy aquarium. Shine a light through it to see it at its best. Then you can eat it!

You Will Need:

Large glass bowl or clear plastic container

3 oz (85 g) packet of blue Jell-O

1 cup (250 ml) hot water

1 1/4 cups (315 ml) cold water

Jelly beans or round gummies

Fish-shaped gummies

Green licorice or twisted candy

1 Ask an adult to help you mix the Jell-O powder with 1 cup of hot water. Add the cold water. You are using more water than listed on the Jello packet to make the Jello a lighter blue.

2 Place some jelly beans or gummies in the bottom of your container to look like gravel. Pour in the Jell-O mixture.

3 Put the container in the fridge for two hours, or until the Jell-O is just beginning to set.

4 Use a butter knife or skewer to make small holes in the Jell-O. Gently put the fish-shaped gummies in some of the holes.

5 Put some green licorice or candy strands in the remaining holes to look like water plants.

6 Return the container to the fridge for another two hours, or until the Jell-O has set.

Did You Know?

Fish breathe by taking oxygen from the water. They take water into their mouths, where it passes over special organs called gills. The gills absorb oxygen from the water, which then passes into the fishes' bloodstream.

The largest fish in the world is the whale shark. It can grow up to 40 feet (12 m) long. That's about the length of a school bus!

Scientists have found that goldfish can be trained to link certain sounds with feeding time. They can even remember these sounds up to five months later.

The smallest fish is a carp that comes from Sumatra, in Indonesia. It is only about 0.3 inch (7.9 mm) long—about the size of your pinky fingernail!

There are tens of thousands of different species of fish in the world today. Scientists are discovering new ones all the time.

Scientists who study fish are called ichthyologists (ICK-thee-ah-lo-jists).

Female seahorses lay their eggs in a pouch on the male's body. The eggs stay in the pouch for about 45 days, until they are ready to hatch.

Fish have been swimming in the oceans for about 450 million years!

Glossary

algae plant or plantlike life-forms that grow mostly in water.

aquarium container, such as a glass tank, for water animals to live in.

aquatic relating to or living in water.

bacteria tiny life-forms that live in soil, water, and living things.

blood worms small, bright red worms used as fish food.

brackish slightly salty.

brine shrimp small shrimp used as fish food.

climate average weather conditions in a place or region over a period of years.

gills feathery parts of the body in fish that take oxygen from water.

iridescent displaying a range of rainbowlike colors.

oxygen gas in the air and water that people and animals need to live.

peaceful (of fish) not aggressive, will not bother tank mates.

siphon tube that uses air pressure to move liquid from one container to another.

sociable liking to be with others.

species group of animals or plants that are similar and are able to produce young.

territorial describes an animal that defends an area.

thermostat device that automatically controls temperature.

tropical occurring in or relating to the tropics— warm areas of the world close to the equator.

vitamin substance usually found in food that animals and people need to live and grow.

Further Resources

Books

Hamilton, Lynn and Katie Gillespie.
Fish (Caring for My Pet),
AV2 by Weigl, 2014.

Niven, Felicia Lowenstein.
Learning to Care for Fish
(Beginning Pet Care with
American Humane), Enslow
Publishers, Inc., 2010.

Richardson, Adele D.
Caring for Your Fish, (Positively
Pets), Capstone Press, 2006.

Websites

Due to the changing nature of Internet links,
PowerKids Press has developed an online list
of websites related to the subject of this
book. This site is updated regularly.
Please use this link to access the list:

www.powerkidslinks.com/cpfk/fish

Index